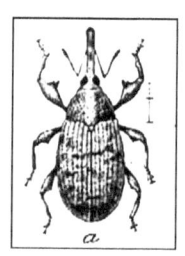

Published by Boll Weevil Press
Newnan, GA
bollweevilpress.com

Copyright © 2017 by Larisa McMichæl

book designed by Dale Lyles

Foreword by Michael Scott

Visitors and newcomers to Newnan are surprised to learn our town uses two currencies. We accept dollars, but if you look closely you will see folks from all walks of life paying for their meals, their car repairs and even their clothes with something else. No, they are not using Bitcoins or Confederate Bonds. They are using gift cards given to them by one of Newnan's best known residents, Mr. Personality.

Newnan is a caring place where people of all colors, incomes and backgrounds look after each other. When Mr. Personality is eating out at any one of Newnan's restaurants or coffee shops it is not unusual for someone, a total stranger, to pick up the tab. Mr. Personality is gracious. Mr. Personality is forever thankful. He frequently returns such thoughtfulness by purchasing a gift card from the shop and surprising someone he knows needs help with the currency of kindness and joy.

You may see Mr. Personality blowing bubbles on the Courthouse Square. You may see him shaking his maracas at a local car lot. You may see him laying some unique dance moves at the Greenville Street Park. Whereever you see him you can be assured of one thing. Mr. Personality is sharing joy and a positive, affirming outlook on life. Newnan is proud to introduce Mr. Personality.

Personality Matters

Believing is everything . . .

Every day I do what I can with what I have.

My job is not a job because I love what I do.

Life is too short to be ordinary.

Children are a joy to the world and our hope for the future.

Strangers are simply friends I have yet to meet.

People who don't read are no better off than people who can't read.

Solitude is an excellent way to know thyself.

Life is one sweet thing after another.

Everybody's got something to bring to the party.

Friendship is the very essence of life and makes it worth living.

End each day with thanksgiving and a grateful heart.

Death is a friend who will escort me off the stage when my act is over.

A Note from Mr. Personality

My Transformation into a "Noonanite" by Mr. Personality

In January 2013, after leaving a town where there was nowhere to go and not much to do for a man on foot, I discovered the Newnan Courthouse Square. It seemed tailor made for me, Mr. Personality.

Within my first 3 days in Newnan I had a job waving a sign for a local business. Divine Spirit and the friendly people of Newnan are still guiding me through an amazing adventure going into my fifth year. Everyday in Newnan is a joy and a blessing. Really it is!

One experience that captured my heart came early when I followed a suggestion to attend the funeral for a man named "Boomer". I never had the pleasure of meeting "Boomer", but the local paper reported many stories of his life and character. I was curious and decided to attend the funeral. It was amazing! By the time I arrived, the Presbyterian church was standing room only with the exception of one seat. Three older ladies insisted that I take it.

From that day on, after seeing how "Boomer" was accepted, my heart belonged to Newnan. It was the right town for me. The acts of kindness I still receive daily is an affirmation of my choice to live in this town. This is a true sign of Divine Spirit's love. Simply put, Newnan is Heaven on Earth.

Come see me on the Courthouse Square for free hugs!!

William Crenshaw, a.k.a. "Mr. Personality" was born in Bloomfield, Missouri, on August 5, 1949. A middle child of five children, he grew up to be a soldier in the Army. Life took many twists and turns. Over the years, as an adult living in Florida, he worked as a small arms instructor, a day laborer, a stock boy, and a dishwasher at Denny's among other occupations. Eventually he decided to change his environment. Georgia was calling. After crossing the border he resolved to forsake cigars and whisky. A higher calling bade him a better existence. What that was, he was not quite sure, but he had once chased lightning bugs in Missouri evenings and smiled at the man in the moon, so he trusted the Divine Spirit would teach him, hold him, bolster him and make him useful.

He checked into a one-room flat in Fayetteville, Georgia, where his alternate persona, "Mr. Personality" incubated for nine months. Never a driver, he walked to shops, the library and the local park. He dressed for joy and people noticed. "Could we offer you a ride? Can we help you?" He doted on those who were happy, who liked him. Others found him uncomfortably odd, even repugnant. Another place beckoned, so onward...

January 2013, Mr. Personality moved into an apartment on Jackson Street in Newnan, Georgia. His first job in town was holding a sign for a business on the bypass. Eventually he found his way to Newnan's town square and his life, the culmination of everything he always wanted it to be, began to come true. Divine Spirit had indeed led him to the work that has become his life's calling. Everyday he awakens with the purpose of making people laugh, smile, and marvel at his fashion sense, helping businesses gain traction with customers, and perhaps, most importantly, promoting Newnan as an amazing place to live and work. He is home. Finally. And he belongs to us all.

Mr. Personality is quick-witted, good-natured, and eager to meet anyone. If ever on the square in downtown Newnan, be sure to get one of his FREE HUGS or a high-five. He listens to everyone, has wisdom to share, and you'll walk away with a smile on your face.

Long live Mr. Personality!

Personality Matters is a collaboration of Mr. Personality and his friend Larisa.

Photos:

cover: The Alamo mural

1 Greenville Street Park
2 Coweta County Courthouse
3 Deals for Dollars
4 Broadway Fashion
5 Boys & Girls Club Gym
6 Shun's Wingyard
7 The Newnan Carnegie Library
8 Leaf 'n' Bean Coffee Shop
9 Candy Vogue
10 Insignia of Newnan Assisted Living Facility
11 La Hacienda Mexican Restaurant
12 Christy's Cafe
13 Temple Avenue
14 Oak Hill Cemetery

bio: The Alamo

back cover: painting by Tracy, age 13

www.ingramcontent.com/pod-product-compliance
Lightning Source LLC
Chambersburg PA
CBHW040734150426
42811CB00063B/1632